SHANTISTAN TABLET:
ENABLING A LAND OF PEACE

To order additional copies of this book, contact:
Xlibris
844-714-8691
www.Xlibris.com
Orders@Xlibris.com

Library of Congress Control Number: 2022912382
ISBN: Softcover 978-1-6698-3636-0
ISBN: EBook 978-1-6698-3637-7

Print information available on the last page

Rev. date: 07/07/2022

SHANTISTAN TABLET
ENABLING LAND OF PEACE

SHANTISTAN TABLET: TABLE OF CONTENTS

SHANTISTAN TABLET

INTRODUCTION

Shantistan Tablet is an addendum to *Shantistan: Enabling a Land of Peace.* (2021), a transculture enrichment program. Thirteen narrative themes are presented and participants are encouraged to apply personal cultural examples.

Each of the *Tablet* concept theme sheets contain theory and methods of peacemaking strategies. These can apply between antagonists, whether they be religious, familial or between communities and nations. *Shantistan Tablet* sheets may be used separately or integrated as steps leading to peace.

Their content integrates language applications to the overall thirteen concept themes. Participants provide brief narratives or concept mapping. Other language applications include paraphrase, interpretation, integration, application, principle extraction and summarization.

Two completed examples are provided at the end.

Example 1: Concept Theme: Sacrifice
Example 2: Mapping Theme: Culture Bearer

Drs. Ruth and Stanley Burgess in Rome.

SHANTISTAN TABLET: *CIVILITY*

"From Decontextual to Contextual Understandings"

1.0

1.1 A definition for CIVILITY is ...

1.2 Identify an incident relating to CIVILITY.

1.3 The following values or wisdom principles relate to this graphic theme.

1.4 Using a past or current experience, relate when you learned about this *Shantistan* theme.

1.5 My culture makes these CIVILITY applications.

1.6 Other extended applications of this *Shantistan* theme are ...

Name: _____ Date: _____

SHANTISTAN TABLET: *DEVOTION TO BELIEFS*

"From Decontextual to Contextual Understandings"

1.0

1.1 A definition for DEVOTION TO BELIEFS is...

1.2 Identify an incident relating to DEVOTION TO BELIEFS.

1.3 The following values or wisdom principles relate to this graphic theme.

1.4 Using a past or current experience, relate when you learned about this *Shantistan* **theme.**

1.5 My culture makes these DEVOTION TO BELIEFS **applications.**

1.6 Other extended applications of this *Shantistan* **theme are ...**

Name: _____ **Date:** _____

SHANTISTAN TABLET: *DOING GOOD*

© Ruth Vassar Burgess 1996, 2020
Distributed by the Burgess Trust

"From Decontextual to Contextual Understandings"

1.0

1.1 A definition for DOING GOOD is ...

1.2 Identify an incident relating to DOING GOOD.

1.3 The following values or wisdom principles relate to this graphic theme.

1.4 Using a past or current experience, relate when you learned about this *Shantistan* theme.

1.5 My culture makes these DOING GOOD applications.

1.6 Other extended applications of this *Shantistan* theme are ...

Name: _____ Date: _____

SHANTISTAN TABLET: *FAITH AND FORGIVENESS*

"From Decontextual to Contextual Understandings"

1.0

1.1 A definition for FAITH AND FORGIVENESS is ...

1.2 Identify an incident relating to FAITH AND FORGIVENESSS.

1.3 The following values or wisdom principles relate to this graphic theme.

1.4 Using a past or current experience, relate when you learned about this *Shantistan* **theme.**

1.5 My culture makes these FAITH AND FORGIVENESS applications.

1.6 Other extended applications of this *Shantistan* **theme are ...**

Name: _____ **Date:** _____

4

SHANTISTAN TABLET: *HARMONY*

"From Decontextual to Contextual Understandings"

1.0

1.1 A definition for HARMONY is...

1.2 Identify an incident relating to HARMONY.

1.3 The following values or wisdom principles relate to this graphic theme.

1.4 Using a past or current experience relate when you learned about this *Shantistan* theme.

1.5 My culture makes these HARMONY applications.

1.6 Other extended applications of this *Shantistan* theme are ...

Name: _____ **Date:** _____

SHANTISTAN TABLET: *HUMAN DIGNITY*

"From Decontextual to Contextual Understandings"

1.0

1.1 A definition for HUMAN DIGNITY is...

1.2 Identify an incident relating to HUMAN DIGNITY.

1.3 The following values or wisdom principles relate to this graphic theme.

1.4 Using a past or current experience, relate when you learned about this *Shantistan* theme.

1.5 My culture makes these HUMAN DIGNITY applications.

1.6 Other extended applications of this *Shantistan* theme are ...

Name: _____ **Date:** _____

SHANTISTAN TABLET: **HUMAN KINDNESS**

"From Decontextual to Contextual Understandings"

1.0

1.1 A definition for HUMAN KINDNESS is...

1.2 Identify an incident relating to HUMAN KINDNESS.

1.3 The following values or wisdom principles relate to this graphic theme.

1.4 Using a past or current experience, relate when you learned about this *Shantistan* theme.

1.5 My culture makes these HUMAN KINDNESS applications.

1.6 Other extended applications of this *Shantistan* theme are ...

Name: _____ Date: _____

SHANTISTAN TABLET: INTEGRITY

"From Decontextual to Contextual Understandings"

1.0

1.1 A definition for INTEGRITY is...

1.2 Identify an incident relating to INTEGRITY.

1.3 The following values or wisdom principles relate to this graphic theme.

1.4 Using a past or current experience, relate when you learned about this *Shantistan* theme.

1.5 My culture makes these INTEGRITY applications.

1.6 Other extended applications of this *Shantistan* theme are ...

Name: _____ Date: _____

SHANTISTAN TABLET: *LOVE*

"From Decontextual to Contextual Understandings"

1.0

1.1 A definition for LOVE is...

1.2 Identify an incident relating to LOVE.

1.3 The following values or wisdom principles relate to this graphic theme.

1.4 Using a past or current experience, relate when you learned about this *Shantistan* theme.

1.5 My culture makes these LOVE applications.

1.6 Other extended applications of this *Shantistan* theme are ...

Name: _____ Date: _____

SHANTISTAN TABLET: *PROTECTION OF LIFE*

"From Decontextual to Contextual Understandings"

1.0

1.1 A definition for PROTECTION OF LIFE is...

1.2 Identify an incident relating to PROTECTION OF LIFE.

1.3 The following values or wisdom principles relate to this graphic theme.

1.4 Using a past or current experience, relate when you learned about this *Shantistan* **theme.**

1.5 My culture makes these PROTECTION OF LIFE applications.

1.6 Other extended applications of this *Shantistan* **theme are ...**

Name: _____ **Date:** _____

SHANTISTAN TABLET: *RECONCILIATION*

"From Decontextual to Contextual Understandings"

1.0

1.1 A definition for RECONCILIATION is ...

1.2 Identify an incident relating to RECONCILIATION.

1.3 The following values or wisdom principles relate to this graphic theme.

1.4 Using a past or current experience, relate when you learned about this *Shantistan* theme.

1.5 My culture makes these RECONCILIATION *applications*

1.6 Other extended applications of this *Shantistan* theme are ...

Name: _____ Date: _____

SHANTISTAN TABLET: *SACRIFICE*

"From Decontextual to Contextual Understandings"

1.0

1.1 A definition for SACRIFICE is ...

1.2 Identify an incident relating to SACRIFICE.

1.3 The following values or wisdom principles relate to this graphic theme.

1.4 Using a past or current experience, relate when you learned about this *Shantistan* **theme.**

1.5 My culture makes these SACRIFICE applications.

1.6 Other extended applications of this *Shantistan* **theme are ...**

Name: _____ **Date:** _____

SHANTISTAN TABLET: *TOLERANCE*

"From Decontextual to Contextual Understandings"

1.0

1.1 A definition for TOLERANCE is...

1.2 Identify an incident relating to TOLERANCE.

1.3 The following values or wisdom principles relate to this graphic theme.

1.4 Using a past or current experience, relate when you learned about this *Shantistan* theme.

1.5 My culture makes these TOLERANCE applications.

1.6 Other extended applications of this *Shantistan* theme are ...

Name: _____ Date: _____

CONCEPT THEME: SACRIFICE

Story

Dear My Teacher, Dr. Stan Burgess,
I would like to say thank you for helping me to rebuild my
life. In my escape from communism I lost relatives and
friends and a lot of things. I appreciate your friendship,
your kindness and your devoted help. I am very
consoled and strengthened by your help.
Refuge Students, Southeast Asia,2001

PARAPHRASE OF CONCEPT (Sacrifice)
Something is forfeited or altered.

INTERPRETATION OF WORD (Sacrifice)
Sacrifice can mean to forfeit something of a greater value for something less.

INTEGRATION OF WORK
To give away at a loss or value.

APPLICATION TO ONE'S VOCABULARY
Our family's social time was less when Dad went to "boot camp."

PRINCIPLE EXTRACTION
Historically there were times when the only solution to a problem was a sacrificial gift.

SUMMARIZATION
A sacrifice may apply differently to different culture groups.

CONCEPT THEME: CULTURE BEARER

GRAPHIC THEME:MAPPING ACCESSABILITY

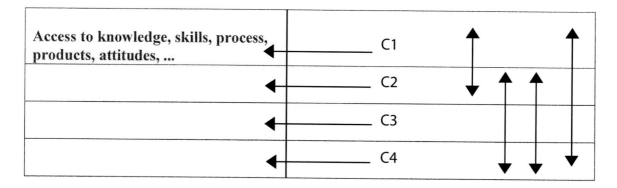

PARAPHRASE
Culture bearers transmit culture icons from person to person and often intergenerationally.

INTERPRETATION
Society may influence broad or narrow accessibility to knowledge, skills and attitudes.

INTEGRATION OF MEANING
Social class systems are enforced when different socio-economic systems are considered "sub-class" or "co-class."

APPLICATION
The culture bearer transmits values, ideas, knowledge and material resources transgenerationally.

PRINCIPLE EXTRACTION
The ability to extract transcendent values supports the development of critical thinking.

SUMMARIZATION
Individuals who treasure and actively use historical and heritage sites, artifacts and narratives become culture bearers.

CONTRIBUTORS

Sophia Burgess contributed her artistic graphic skills to the Shantistan cover. See below.

Elizabeth Dotson contributed her artistry to the Shantistan Quilt which is displayed on this Stantistan Tablet front cover.

Mark Shipley added his graphic skills to this production.

Marketplace Printing and Design contributed to the layout and printing of this book.

Ruth Vassar Burgess, *Shantistan: Enabling a Land of Peace.*
West Bow Press, Bloomington, IN: 2020.

Printed in the United States
by Baker & Taylor Publisher Services